Friends Till the End?

a quiz book for *a smart girl's guide:*
friendship troubles

by Emma MacLaren Henke
illustrated by Angela Martini

Published by American Girl Publishing
Copyright © 2013 by American Girl

Questions or comments? Call 1-800-845-0005,
visit **americangirl.com**, or write to Customer Service,
American Girl, 8400 Fairway Place, Middleton, WI 53562-0497.

Printed in China
13 14 15 16 17 18 19 20 LEO 10 9 8 7 6 5 4 3 2 1

Editor: Trula Magruder
Art Direction & Design: Sarah Boecher
Production: Tami Kepler, Judith Lary, Paula Moon, Kendra Schluter
Illustrations: Angela Martini

Special thanks to Patti Kelley Criswell

Dear Reader,

Friendships make life brighter. But what happens when problems crop up between friends? What do you do if your friends don't treat you with respect? How do you address tricky topics? How do you know if a friend is a good match?

We've filled this book with quizzes to help you solve these and other friendship problems. Inside, you'll discover tips on how to treat your friends, how to deal with bullies, how to be a great friend, and more. Whether you're looking for advice, insight, or just plain fun, you'll find a quiz that's right for you!

Your friends at American Girl

Table of Contents

All About Friends

What do you look for in a friend?
What do your friends see in you?

What's Your Friendship Style?

Take this quiz to discover what kinds of friendships are the best fits for you.

1. I'm the kind of girl who . . .
   a. spends tons of time with one best friend.
   b. wants friends who share my interests.
   c. feels most comfortable in a crowd of friends.

2. I value my friends because . . .
   a. they're there when I need them.
   b. they make me feel as if I belong.
   c. they love to have fun!

3. When I'm getting to know a new friend, I . . .
   a. share my deepest secrets.
   b. like to learn about each other slowly—friendship takes time to grow.
   c. keep conversations light and friendly.

4. I would compare friendship to . . .

a. a snuggly blanket: you can relax around true friends, and they're warm and comforting.

b. a seesaw: friendship has its ups and downs, and you have to work together to have fun.

c. a party: the more friends, the merrier!

5. I'm a good friend because . . .

a. I support my friends no matter what, and I'm a good listener.

b. I love to get involved in activities my friends and I both enjoy.

c. I know how to make sure everyone has a fun time together.

Answers

If you chose mostly **a's,** you look to your friends for advice and support. You're steadfast and loyal, and you love your friends like family.

If you picked lots of **b's,** you enjoy friends who share your passions. When you're doing an activity you love with a friend, your relationship grows.

Did you choose mostly **c's?** For you, friendship equals fun. You like to have a group of friends for sharing laughs and good times.

The next time you have a problem with a friend, think about the kind of relationship you have with her. Then think about what being friends might mean to her. Are you on the same page? Don't worry if you and a pal see friendship differently. It's good to know where you stand when you work to solve your problem together.

Make New Friends

Looking for a new friend? What kind of person would you like her to be? Read all the statements and choose the ones that best describe the kind of friend you'd want to make.

☐ Every time you take your dog to the park for a nice hike, you run into Brita. One day she and her pooch join you, and you talk for your whole walk about how much you both love dogs.

☐ When your soccer team makes it to the championship game, Zina is there to cheer you on, even though she doesn't know the first thing about sports.

☐ You meet Amaya in Japanese class. When she asks you if you'd like to join her family for a sushi dinner, you say, "That sounds great," even though you've never tried raw fish.

☐ Your mom gets a new job. It's exciting—you might be moving to Brazil for a year! When you tell Hannah your news, she says how happy she is for your family and promises not to tell anyone until you know for sure.

☐ You meet Jillian at auditions for *The Nutcracker*, and then you see her again at the first session of your new ballet class. You two must both love to dance.

☐ You love to sing, but you're really afraid to try out for the solo in choir. Aniya tells you that you have a beautiful voice. She helps you practice and sends you a big smile as you give the solo a shot.

☐ You're bored with school, piano lessons, and tennis. So when Jazmin calls you and says, "My dad's taking me to the rock-climbing gym. Want to come along?" you jump at the chance to try something new.

☐ You can't believe you got a D on your history exam. You don't know what went wrong. When Jayla sits next to you on the bus ride home, she can see you're upset and asks, "What's wrong?" As you tell her what happened, she listens thoughtfully without interrupting.

Which color did you choose?

Did you pick **purple?** You might be looking for a friend who shares your interests. Take part in an activity you love with a friend. Having a partner in your pastime can encourage you to learn more, do more, and love it more.

Did you go with **blue?** You'd relish a friend who supports you no matter what. Success feels better shared with a friend. Want a pal who encourages you? Cheer *her* on. She'll likely return the favor, and your accomplishments will be doubly sweet.

Did you opt for **orange?** You could be searching for a friend who will lead you to new experiences. On your own, try something new you've always wanted to do. You may meet an adventurous new friend along the way!

Did you react to **red?** You're craving a friend who is a great listener. Look for a sympathetic pal with whom you can share your problems. One way to attract a friend who listens to you is to be a good listener yourself.

Tried and True

Some friendships last through thick and thin, but others may not be meant for the long haul. Under each statement, write the names of one or two of your friends who could fit the description.

After we spend time together, I feel good about myself.

_____

_____

Sometimes, after I spend time with this friend, I feel upset.

_____

_____

I love to share good news with this friend—I know she'll be happy for me.

_____

_____

Sometimes I don't share my good news with this friend because I'm afraid she'll be jealous of me.

_____

_____

If we're hanging out—watching a movie, playing, exercising—and we don't talk a lot, that's OK. It still feels easy to spend time together.

_____

_____

When we run out of things to say to each other, it can feel weird to spend time with this friend.

_____

_____

We take turns making decisions about what we'll do together. We're good at compromising.

_____

_____

When I'm with this friend, we always do what she wants to do. I don't complain—it's not worth arguing.

_____

_____

I can be myself around this friend. I'd never be embarrassed if she saw me crying my eyes out or laughing like crazy.

_____

_____

I'm careful how I act around this friend. She'll make fun of me later if I do something silly in front of her.

_____

_____

This friend brings out the best in me.

_____

_____

I don't always make my best choices or act like the nicest person when I'm with this friend.

_____

_____

I always try to help out if this friend has a problem or cheer her up if she feels sad.

_____

_____

I'm not sure I want to get involved in this friend's problems.

_____

_____

Answers

Take a look at the names you wrote in the blue-green frames. These are the friends you can count on—your true friends. Treasure and take care of these friendships.

Now check out the names in the red frames. While no friendship is perfect, if you see a name here once or twice, think about how you can work with that friend to solve the problems you might be having. But if you see a name in the red a bunch of times, this may not be a great friendship for you. It's OK to talk to this friend casually, but the two of you may no longer fit in a close relationship.

R-e-s-p-e-c-t

Respect is the glue that holds friendships together. Are you respectful to your friends? Think about how you would handle each of the situations described below. Then mark with a plus sign the ones that you think show respect. Mark the others with a minus sign.

1. You plan to meet your friend at the movies, but she doesn't show up. She calls later to apologize and says that her dad got stuck at work and couldn't drive her to the theater. You stay mad at her for a week.

2. You and your friend both try out for the softball team. She makes the squad, but you don't. You still cheer her on and ask about her first game.

3. You work with a friend on your science-fair project. Her part of the experiment is a complete flop. You don't get mad at her, though, because you know she tried her best.

4. Your friend wants you to go bird-watching with her and her mom. They're crazy about birds, but you can't tell a sparrow from a stork. You go along anyway and try to listen and learn.

5. Your friend borrows your shirt and gets a stain on it. You complain to all your other friends that she's a slob.

6. Your friend really loves a new band and wants you to hear their hit song. You know you'll hate it, and you roll your eyes and make a sour face as the music plays.

Respect

7. Your friend gets funky new glasses. You're not sure you'd like them for yourself, but you tell her that the new specs really suit her cool style.

8. You promise to help your friend study for the math test—it's not her best subject, and you're a math whiz. Your brother asks if you'd like to go to the pool with him at the same time you planned to study with your friend. You skip the pool, even though you love to swim.

Answers

Situations 1, 5, and 6 are examples of ways you might be disrespectful to your friends. All the rest describe ways you could show respect for a friend.

Respecting a friend means you're considerate of her. You believe in her, and you take her apologies as sincere. You try to be happy when your friend succeeds, even if you feel jealous. You don't say mean things behind her back. You're open to your friend's ideas and beliefs and to trying new experiences with her.

Respect is a two-way street. If you treat a friend with respect, she'll treat you the same way. That's a sure path to a wonderful friendship.

Friendship Hot Spots

How do you handle sticky situations
with your friends?

The Best or the Rest?

Some girls want a best friend—someone special to love and support, someone who will listen to their worries. Take a look at the actions described below. Circle the B if you think a best friend would do it. Circle the R if it's something a best friend would not do.

Is a best friend someone who . . .

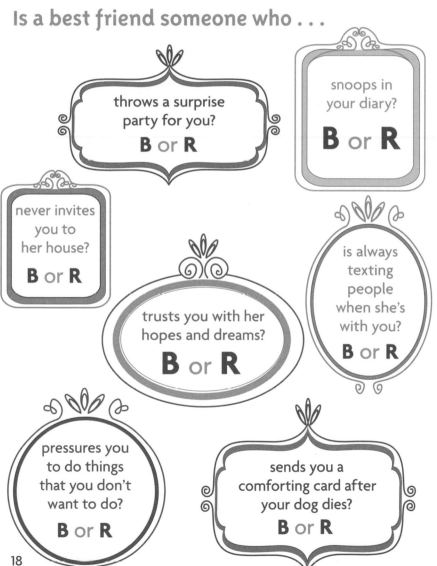

throws a surprise party for you?
B or **R**

snoops in your diary?
B or **R**

never invites you to her house?
B or **R**

trusts you with her hopes and dreams?
B or **R**

is always texting people when she's with you?
B or **R**

pressures you to do things that you don't want to do?
B or **R**

sends you a comforting card after your dog dies?
B or **R**

gives you a hug when you need one?
B or **R**

stands up to a bully who picks on you?
B or **R**

cries in front of you?
B or **R**

makes fun of you?
B or **R**

laughs at your jokes?
B or **R**

sits in the front row when you're in the school play?
B or **R**

tells your secret to the whole class?
B or **R**

Take a look at your answers—they'll tell you a lot about what you expect from a best friend. The acts that you circled R's for are betrayals you wouldn't want from any friend. But remember that no one is perfect, and no friendship is perfect, either.

19

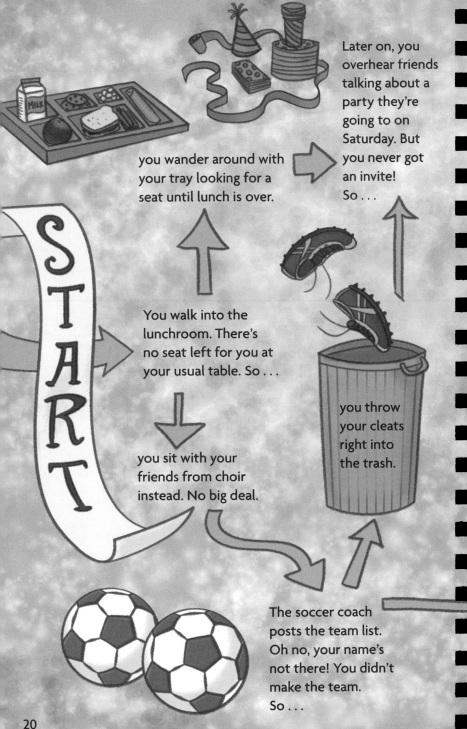

you wander around with your tray looking for a seat until lunch is over.

Later on, you overhear friends talking about a party they're going to on Saturday. But you never got an invite! So . . .

You walk into the lunchroom. There's no seat left for you at your usual table. So . . .

you throw your cleats right into the trash.

you sit with your friends from choir instead. No big deal.

The soccer coach posts the team list. Oh no, your name's not there! You didn't make the team. So . . .

you act as if you were invited, too. But you stay home crying on Saturday night.

you just keep quiet and try not to act upset.

You had plans to go to the mall with a friend, but she canceled at the last minute. You still go shopping with your mom, and you spot your friend in line at the movies with another girl. You decide that . . .

your friend must care only about trying to be popular. Some friend she is!

Getting left out feels lousy! But if you can recover gracefully when you get the brush-off, you'll look confident and strong. Try not to let small slights ruin your perspective on the big picture.

you call a friend from another school and make plans to see a movie that night.

you'd rather work alone. Their history grades aren't exactly up to your standards for project partners, anyway.

you'll check in with your friend at school. But there's no point in ruining your shopping trip by being upset.

Everyone feels left out once in a while. But you know that usually it's not personal. Not every small snub has to cause a big problem.

you hit the basketball court instead. You really just want to get some exercise.

You're chatting online with a few friends. They're planning to work together on a project for history class—but they don't ask you to join their group. You decide . . .

they must have heard you explaining your idea to research covered wagons. They want to build a model of a one-room schoolhouse.

MOVIE 12
FUNHOUSE 4
4:20 PM
4:20 PM

On the Outside

Do you ever feel left out? Ignored? Pushed around? Follow this fun flowchart to see how you handle the times when you don't fit in.

Are You Too Jealous?

Take this quiz to find out if you're overly jealous or mostly carefree.

1. You and your friend Seema both audition for a solo in choir. Seema gets the part, but you really wanted it. You tell your other friends, "Seema's not that great of a singer. She got the part because she's the teacher's favorite."

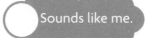
Sounds like me.　　That's not me.

2. You and your friend Beth both love basketball, but Beth is the team's star and you spend a lot of time on the bench. You'd love to be a better player, so you ask Beth if she can give you some tips after practice.

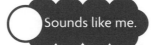
Sounds like me.　　That's not me.

3. Desiree, your pal from dance class, got a new smart phone. She spends every break from rehearsal texting friends and snapping funny photos. You'd love your own phone, but your parents say no. You complain to your dance teacher that Desiree is spending too much time on her phone and not enough time working on her steps.

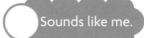
Sounds like me.　　That's not me.

4. You were dying to go horseback riding at Brielle's grandmother's horse ranch, but your parents don't want you to travel that far away. You adore horses, so you promise Brielle that you'll text her a lot and make her swear to text back and send you pics of the horses.

22  Sounds like me.　　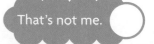 That's not me.

5. You, Gabby, and her aunt have tickets to see your favorite band in concert. At the last minute, you get sick, and your mom says you can't go. Gabby takes another pal instead. The next day, you tell them both that the band they saw is for babies. Cool kids are into the next thing now.

◯ Sounds like me.   That's not me. ◯

6. You study hard for your biology test, and you get a B+. You're feeling great until you see that your friend Brittany got 100%—again! You know that she spent the night before the exam catching up on her favorite TV show. She told you all about it. You congratulate Brittany anyway.

◯ Sounds like me.   That's not me. ◯

Answers

If you chose mostly **red** answers, you have jealousy under control. You know that everyone feels jealous once in a while. You understand the difference between things you want and things you need, and you know that friendships are more important than a new gadget, starring role, or fancy trip.

If you chose mostly **green** answers, jealousy gets the best of you sometimes. When you feel jealous that on spring break a friend gets to go to an amusement park while you're visiting your grouchy aunt, try admitting your emotion. Tell her, "I'm really happy for you, but I feel kind of jealous, too. I wish it were me." Then change the subject. Your friend will understand—she feels jealous sometimes, too!

Winner Take All?

Friends work together to do what's best for their relationship—right? Not always. From the struggle to keep up with a friend to the urge to take charge, difficult emotions can make it hard to maintain an equal balance of power. See how you handle the competition in your friendships.

1. You and Cinda both love to play games. When she spends the night at your house, you plan an evening of cards and board games. After she wins both Crazy Eights and checkers, you . . .
   a. congratulate Cinda and ask her what she'd like to do next. She is the guest, after all.
   b. tell her that she must be pretty lucky today. Then make her play your new video game—the one that you've mastered but you know she's never tried.
   c. run up to your room and slam the door. How dare she win at your house!

2. You and Rebekah have been close friends since first grade. At camp this summer, you both started hanging out with a new girl named Julia. When Julia asks Rebekah to be her locker partner for the school year, Rebekah agrees. You . . .
   a. are hurt that Rebekah chose the new girl to partner with, but you also know that Rebekah always makes people feel welcome.
   b. wish Rebekah had checked with you first—the two of you were locker partners last year.
   c. tell them both they're too messy to share a locker with anyway.

25

3. You and your pal Marissa are both trying out for the lead in the school musical. You . . .

   a. rehearse together before your auditions. You hope you can help each other find the best way to interpret the part.

   b. don't talk to Marissa until you find out if one of you gets the role—until then, it's too tense.

   c. refuse to accept a part in the chorus after Marissa gets the lead.

4. You've been figure skating for a few years. You love it! Then your friend Tamia takes up skating, and she's really good. You'll be competing against each other. You . . .

   a. pledge to cheer each other on, no matter what.

   b. tell Tamia she's doing great—then practice as much as you can so that you'll have the best chance to beat her.

   c. ignore Tamia at the rink. She should know that skating is your thing.

5. You and your friend Ciara both have a crush on Toby. When you're with Ciara, you . . .

   a. spend tons of time talking about how nice Toby is and how great he is at soccer.

   b. tell Ciara you're sure you'll get to be lab partners with Toby. You have science class with him, but she does not.

   c. tell Ciara that Toby would never go for a tomboy like her.

6. A poem you wrote is selected for the school's literary journal. You're really proud! You worked hard on that poem. When you find out a story by your best friend Merritt will be in the journal, too, you . . .

   a. ask her if she wants to go out for ice cream to celebrate.

   b. have a hard time telling Merritt you loved her story, even though you couldn't put it down when you were reading it.

   c. hint that Merritt stole the idea for her story from a movie you watched together, even though it's not true.

Scoring

Give yourself 2 points for each a you chose, 1 point for each b, and 0 points for each c. Add up your score.

8 or more points

Great Sport

You don't let competition come between you and your friends. You support a friend and hope she does her best, even when she's competing against you. Everyone likes to win, but you know that friendships are more important than being in first place.

4 to 7 points

Position Player

You sometimes let your desire to win or to get attention come between you and your friends. Deep down, you want your pals to do their best. But you might get a bit jealous when they do things as well as you.

0 to 3 points

Rough Rival

You might be quite competitive. But don't let that get in the way of your friendships. Competition is a great motivator, but really, you can only do your best. And remember, when a friend succeeds, it doesn't mean that you fail.

It's Tricky

Read the puzzling problems described below. Then explain how you'd handle each one. Answer these questions alone or with your friends.

1. You don't see your best friend, Raven, much over the summer because you're away on a family trip. A new girl, Celeste, moves in on Raven's street. When school starts, Raven and Celeste are acting as if they've been best friends forever.
What would you do?

_____

_____

_____

2. You're good friends with Greg, but your other friends tease you for hanging out with him and say he's your boyfriend.
What would you do?

_____

_____

_____

3. Every time something good happens for you, something great seems to happen for your friend Kristine. You make the volleyball team. She's elected team captain. You get an A in science. She wins the science fair. You have a sleepover at your house. She invites your friends to an overnight party at a hotel with a water park.
What would you do?

_____

_____

_____

4. All your friends text on their cell phones and get to chat online, but your parents won't let you do either. You feel left out. What would you do?

_____

_____

_____

5. Celia invites you to go hiking with her family on Saturday, and then Angela asks you to take a pottery class with her. You'd love to do both. What would you do?

_____

_____

_____

Here are some ideas for how you could handle the tricky situations from the previous pages. Remember, though, that even if these are different from your answers, what you wrote isn't necessarily wrong. You can tackle tough spots in many different ways.

1. Instead of feeling jealous of Celeste, try to make friends with her. If your best friend likes her, she's probably great. Invite Raven and Celeste to do something with you together. There's no limit to the number of friends you can have.

2. It's good to have different kinds of friends. The next time your friends bug you about Greg, casually say, "Greg's a great friend, just like you guys." Don't make it a big deal and your friends won't either.

3. There'll always be friends who are smarter, richer, or luckier than you—it's life! And while feeling jealous of that success can be normal, resenting it can quickly poison a friendship. Instead, view your friendships as partnerships. Then when a friend is successful, you'll feel successful, too!

4. Don't beg or whine, but let your parents know that you're feeling left out because kids text on cell phones and chat online. Then, even if your parents don't change their minds, you've made them aware of your frustrations. Also, remind your friends that you're not in the digital loop. Kindly ask them to contact you the old-fashioned way—by calling your home phone. Say it with a laugh and a smile, and your friends will understand.

5. Did you tell either friend you'd go with her? If you did, keep your promise and apologize to your other friend. Say that you'd love to come but you have other plans. If you didn't, choose what you'd like to do most. Then tell the other friend that you can't make it, but you'd love to do something fun together soon.

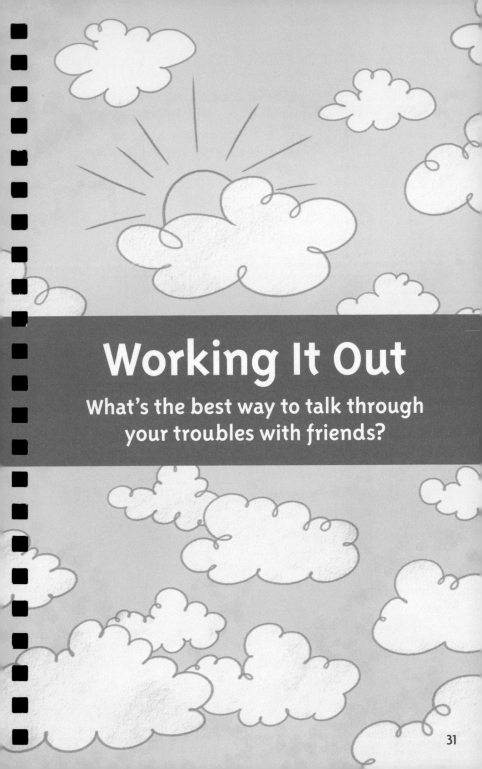

Working It Out

What's the best way to talk through
your troubles with friends?

When Life Gives You Lemons

Make lemonade! Every friendship has its share of problems. Did you know that you can use those problems to make your friendships even stronger? Take a look at the situations below, and then try to spot the opportunity in each friendship crisis.

1. Your pal is a perfectionist on group projects. You love her, but you don't want to work with her anymore.
Here's a chance to . . .

   a. complain to your teacher that you have too many group projects. You'd rather work alone!
   b. compliment your friend as you bow out of the project. Tell her what an awesome job she does on school projects. Then say you can't spend as much time on the project as you know she'd want you to.
   c. act really bossy until your friend lets you do the next project your way.

2. Your friend always makes up stories about crazy things she's done. You know she's lying, though. You don't understand why she tries to make her life seem more exciting than it is.
Here's a chance to . . .

   a. let all your other friends know that this friend is a big liar.
   b. make up some stories of your own—you've been feeling as if your life is pretty dull too.
   c. talk to your friend about trust. Say you have a feeling that she's not telling the truth sometimes, and you value trust in a friendship. Then tell her you love her just as she is—she doesn't need to impress you.

3. Your friend got a new dog, and it's all she talks about. You really want a dog, but your parents won't let you have one. It's driving you crazy.

Here's a chance to . . .

a. let her know you're happy that she has a new dog but that it's hard for you, since you want a dog so badly. Ask if you can spend time with her dog when you're together—maybe you could both take her pet to the park. Then gently change the subject.

b. tell her that you've changed your mind about dogs—her dog sounds so awful, you'd never want one now.

c. talk all about your new laptop. Your friend is dying for a computer, but her parents think she's too young.

4. You're mad at your friend because you feel as if she never listens to you. She talks and talks when you're together, but when you have something to say, she interrupts you.

Here's a chance to . . .

a. get your friend's attention and tell her nicely how you feel. Let her know that you love hearing what she has to say but that you'd like to talk about yourself some, too.

b. give your friend the silent treatment. That will show her what it feels like to be ignored!

c. give her a piece of your mind. You have to yell to get through to her, right?

5. You're camping with your friend. She was no help at all when you put up your tent, and you screamed at her. Now you feel awful about it.

Here's a chance to . . .

a. keep away from her for the rest of the camping trip. You'd like to get closer with a few other girls anyway.

b. make fun of your friend when she stinks at starting a fire, too.

c. apologize sincerely. You know it's the right thing to do, and you don't want the rest of the trip to be spoiled.

Problems between friends give you the chance to put the golden rule into action: treat others as you would like to be treated. If you keep that rule in mind, you can turn setbacks into strengths.

1. b, 2. c, 3. a, 4. a, 5. c

Answers

What's Bugging You?

Sometimes when you fight with a friend, the words you say don't really show how you're feeling. When you have a conflict with a friend, try answering these questions together. Perhaps your answers will help you get to the bottom of your problem.

1. What happened in our disagreement? What did I say? What did you say?

2. Did I accurately describe what's making me upset? If not, what's really on my mind?

3. What do I think is making you upset?

4. Is there anything I'd like to apologize for?

5. Will I still be upset about this tomorrow? In a week? Will you be upset then?

Take some time to talk through your answers together. Make sure to listen to what your friend says.

Remember, it's OK to feel angry at a friend. If you feel too angry to work with your friend, answer these questions by yourself as you take some time to cool down. Be honest about how you feel. Then find a way to talk to your friend.

1. What happened in our disagreement? What did I say? What did you say?

_____

_____

2. Did I accurately describe what's making me upset? If not, what's really on my mind?

_____

3. What do I think is making you upset?

_____

4. Is there anything I'd like to apologize for?

_____

5. Will I still be upset about this tomorrow? In a week? Will you be upset then?

_____

Take some time to talk through your answers together. Make sure to listen to what your friend says.

Remember, it's OK to feel angry at a friend. If you feel too angry to work with your friend, answer these questions by yourself as you take some time to cool down. Be honest about how you feel. Then find a way to talk to your friend.

Let It Go or Just Say No?

Sometimes friends can hurt your feelings without meaning to do anything wrong. But once in a while, friends don't have the best intentions. Then you have to speak up! Take this quiz to see if you know when to say when. Circle the answer that suits you best.

1. Your friend really loves your new jacket, and she begs you to let her borrow it. When you tell her, "No, I just got it," she says she'll tell the whole school about your secret crush if you don't let her wear the jacket.

Let it go.   Just say no.

2. At the last minute, your friend cancels your plans for a movie night together because her out-of-town uncle makes an unplanned visit.

Let it go.   Just say no.

3. In the lunch line, you trip and flip your pizza slice right onto your science teacher. Your friend laughs as she describes to everyone at the lunch table how foolish you looked.

> **Let it go.**   Just say no.

4. Your friend borrows your headphones to listen to music on the bus ride home. The next day, she tells you that her little brother broke them. She apologizes and promises to buy you a new pair as soon as her dad can take her to the store.

> **Let it go.**   Just say no.

5. The movie you're seeing with a good friend gets out earlier than you expected. Your friend wants to walk to the mall even though your mom told you not to leave the theater. When you say no, your friend says, "You're a big baby, and your mom is just a jerk anyway."

> **Let it go.**   Just say no.

6. Your friend says she'll beat you up if you ever tell anyone that she failed her English test.

> **Let it go.**   Just say no.

7. You call your friend three times on Saturday morning trying to make plans for Saturday night, but she never returns your call. Later, she says she was at her sister's soccer game and didn't get your message.

> **Let it go.**   Just say no.

8. Whenever your friend comes over to your house, she heads straight for your computer. She chats online the whole time you're together! She always says the Internet isn't working at her house.

> **Let it go.**   Just say no.

Answers

1. Just say no. It's never OK for a friend to threaten you. Calmly tell your friend that she's making you feel as if she cares more about your stuff than she does about you.

2. Let it go. Your friend has a good reason for the change of plans. Be understanding when something beyond a friend's control means that she has to let you down.

3. Just say no. It's not OK for a friend to embarrass you on purpose. Ask her to stop, and tell her privately that she hurt your feelings.

4. Let it go. Accept your friend's sincere apologies. She didn't mean to break something that belongs to you.

5. Just say no. It's never OK for friends to say mean things about your family or to pressure you to do things you feel uncomfortable doing.

6. Just say no. It's never OK for a friend to threaten you or to hurt you in any way. Tell an adult if you get hurt or if you think that your friend might injure you.

7. Let it go. Trust your friend. We all get busy sometimes.

8. Just say no. Kindly steer your friend toward plans that won't allow her to race for the computer every time she visits.

Time to Talk

Talking about touchy subjects with friends can be difficult. But sometimes you have to talk to get to the bottom of a problem. Take a look at the friendship problems on the next two pages. Match each problem with a reply you might use to address that situation with your friend.

1. My friend is always late to class after lunch because she needs to get something from her locker, ask someone something, or get a drink—and because I'm with her, I'm late, too!

2. Every year a friend asks me why I don't have a Christmas tree.

3. My friend teased me about my new haircut in front of our teacher, and it embarrassed me.

4. When my friend comes over, she never helps clean up before she has to leave.

5. My friend always asks me about my grades, but I like to keep them private.

6. My friend often tries to talk to me during class, but I need to concentrate.

a. "Sorry. I need to pay attention or I'll fall behind."

b. "I'm doing fine. I just try to do my best."

c. "I don't celebrate Christmas. My family celebrates Hanukkah."

d. "Your mom will be here any minute, and I really need to clean up now. My dad gets mad when I leave my things scattered around the house. Could you help me pick up?"

f. "Hey, do you keep time with a sundial? I'm going to go ahead and meet you in class."

e. "You humiliated me in front of Mr. Killian today, and I'm pretty upset."

Answers

1. f. Using humor might ease a tense situation and help your friend see that you're uncomfortable about being late.

2. c. Don't make a big deal about your differences and she won't either.

3. e. If your friend means to hurt your feelings, you need to talk to her or you'll end up resenting her.

4. d. The next time your friend comes over, find out when she has to leave. Then 15 minutes before that time, ask for her help.

5. b. Tell her politely but firmly that you really don't want to compare grades.

6. a. Tell your friend in a nice way that you need to pay attention during class, but you'd love to talk to her at lunch.

Note: Whatever problem you want to bring up, be honest about your feelings. Gather your courage, keep your tone friendly, and speak your mind. Then really listen to what your friend says, too.

What's Your Sorry Style?

How do you act when you need to say you're sorry? To find out how your apologies might make your friends feel, choose the responses that sound most like you.

1. You borrow your pal Bridget's pen and then you lose it. You say,
- **a.** "Hey, I lost your pen. Give me another one, OK?"
- **b.** "Sorry. I lost your pen. But it was out of ink anyway."
- **c.** "I lost the pen I borrowed from you. Sorry! Here—please take this one to replace it."

2. You forget Jaiden's birthday completely. When it was your birthday, she gave you a handmade card and a balloon in the shape of a dolphin, your favorite animal. You say,
- **a.** "Happy late birthday. Too bad you missed your chance for a birthday pinch!"
- **b.** "I'm sorry I missed your birthday. I was really busy, and you didn't make a big deal about it, so I just forgot."
- **c.** "I just realized that I completely forgot your birthday. I'm so sorry! I hope you had a great day." Then you surprise Jaiden with a pretty cupcake.

3. Alice makes you promise not to tell anyone that her parents a re splitting up. When Cara, another friend, confides that she's worried because her parents fight all the time, you blurt out, "You should talk to Alice. She's in the same situation." You tell Alice,
- **a.** "I told Cara about your mom and dad, but I knew you wouldn't care. Her parents are splitting up, too."
- **b.** "I told Cara about your parents. Sorry. I just forgot it was a secret. I don't know why it's so private."
- **c.** "I need to apologize to you. I accidentally told Cara about what's going on with your parents. But I know she could use your advice right now. You're a great friend—you're so thoughtful."

4. At Alina's birthday party, you burp loudly at the table—in front of her grandma!
You say,

   a. nothing. Instead, you look away as if it wasn't you.

   b. "Uh-oh. I guess I ate too much birthday cake," and you giggle.

   c. "Excuse me, please."

5. Penelope asks if you like her room, and you shout, "It looks really messy!"
You say,

   a. "Sorry, but the truth hurts."

   b. "Sorry, but I just like to keep my room really clean."

   c. "Wow. Did I just say that? That was rude. Sorry!"

Answers

Mostly a's
You don't like to apologize, and you try to get by with making a joke or a snarky comment instead. When you know you're in the wrong, don't act as if what you did never happened. If you own up to your mistakes with sincerity and politeness, your friends are more likely to forgive you.

Mostly b's
You know when you've done or said the wrong thing, but you tend to make excuses for your behavior. Your apologies usually come with a "but." Think about how you feel when someone apologizes to you that way. Take responsibility for your mistakes without conditions. Doing so shows respect to your friends—and they're likely to return that respect to you.

Mostly c's
You know how to make an apology that is sincere and meaningful. Your friends must appreciate that you own up to your mistakes without a fuss. You're a saying-sorry role model!

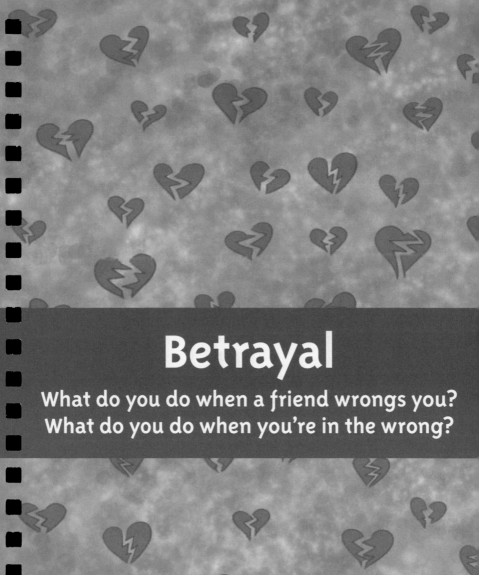

Betrayal

What do you do when a friend wrongs you?
What do you do when you're in the wrong?

Can You Keep a Secret?

Trust is an important building block in any friendship. Answer these questions to find out if you know when to keep your lips zipped.

1. Beth Ann invites you to a sleepover at her house. You're thrilled, but only a few of your friends are also invited to the party. You'd probably . . .

   a. talk about the party all day at school. You're so excited, there's no way you can keep this private.

   b. talk about the party when you're with other girls who have been invited and you're sure no one else will hear.

2. Dominique tells you that she read her sister's diary. "She just leaves it lying around. Want to read it with me the next time you're over?" You'd say . . .

   a. "OK! I'd love to read what she really thinks about that goofy boyfriend of hers!"

   b. "Did she say it was OK? That seems like something she'd want to keep private."

3. Lydia tells you that she has a crush on Teddy, your next-door neighbor. You'd probably . . .

   a. grab Teddy after school to tell him that Lydia is in love with him, and then say, "Oooooo!" for everyone to hear.

   b. keep the news to yourself. You know Lydia told you about her crush in confidence.

4. Valeria tells you that her dad is really sick. He might need to have an operation, and she's very scared. You'd probably . . .
  a. tell your three best friends what's going on with Valeria so that you can work together to help her through this rough time.
  b. ask Valeria if you can talk to other friends about what's going on with her dad. You're sure all your friends would want to help out if they knew.

5. Your mom leaves her Christmas list on the kitchen table, and you see what she bought for your brother: the new video game he's been begging for. You would . . .
  a. run to your brother's room to tell him what you saw. You know he's dying for that game!
  b. keep what you saw to yourself. You don't want to spoil your mom's big surprise.

Answers

If your answers are mostly a's:
You leak information like a broken faucet. That might not seem to matter for small stuff, but trust is important in a friendship. By sharing a friend's news without permission—even if the news is good or even if you know she needs help—you can damage that trust. The next time you want to spout a friend's secret, remind yourself that people don't always respect the person spreading the news.

If your answers are mostly b's:
You understand that when a friend shares something private with you, she's showing you that she trusts you. And you know that private information you find out by accident is not yours to share. Your lips are sealed.

Now that you're done taking the quiz, answer the questions with one of your friends in mind. What do you think she would do in each situation? Your responses might give you a hint about whether you can share your own secrets with her.

Important: Sometimes you have to tell a secret. If you hear a secret that makes you think a friend might be in danger or in serious trouble, tell an adult you trust right away. Safety is more important than keeping a confidence.

Buddy or Backstabber?

Take a look at the statements below. Put a check next to each one you might say behind a friend's back.

I can't believe Carmen's wearing that sweater! She looks like my grandma.

I'd never let my mom cut my hair. Felice looks awful.

Yay! Ann got elected class president. I voted for her!

When Megan reads to herself, her lips move. Can you believe it?

I really love Kym's new backpack. I wonder where she got it.

Bianca failed another test. Do you think she's going to get held back this year? I bet she has to go to summer school.

Evie's dad lost his job. I bet they'll have to move. Their house is huge! It must have cost a lot of money.

I wish I had hair like Sydney's.

Zoe wore the same jeans to school every day this week. That's gross.

Riley spent the night at my house, and she still sucks her thumb in her sleep. It was hilarious!

52

Now look at the statements again. Put a plus sign next to each one you'd say behind a friend's back if you knew it would get back to her. Then compare your checks and pluses. Do they overlap?

The statements on the three green flags are the only ones that don't betray a friend in one way or another. Saying mean things about friends behind their backs is disloyal and dishonest. Before you speak about a friend, always assume that what you say will get back to her. Then think about the kind of things you'd like your friends to say about you.

If you're sure a friend has been saying nasty things about you, confront her. Don't try to second-guess what's going on. Get to the bottom of the problem politely, in private. It's important for your friends to respect your feelings.

Is This Friendship Over?

Not all friendships last forever. Do you add anything positive to your friend's life? Does she add to yours? If not, it may be time to call it quits. Think of a friend you're having a hard time with, and then put a check next to each statement that could describe your friendship.

☐ Sometimes I do cruel things to this friend on purpose.

☐ I hang out with this friend only because I feel as if I'm supposed to. I don't want to be mean.

☐ If my phone rings and I see the call is from this friend, I rarely pick it up.

☐ Sometimes I say hurtful things about this friend to my other friends.

☐ It seems as if this friend never really listens to me, even when I'm telling her something important.

☐ I don't look forward to spending time with this friend.

☐ Everything I do with this friend turns into a competition. I'm sick of it!

☐ Secretly, I feel happy when something bad happens to this friend.

☐ I don't really pay attention when this friend talks.

55

Answers

If you marked one or two statements, think about ways you could work out your problems with this friend. Perhaps you just need to create a few rules or boundaries about how you'll act when you're together.

If you marked more than two statements, it may be time to redefine your friendship so that you have less contact with this person—for now at least. Be kind. Let your friendship cool for a while. Avoid spending time together outside of school, and put some distance between you and your friend. You can still talk to each other casually. Just because you're not a great match doesn't mean you need to hate each other. Who knows? In a few months, you might find that you have more in common than you do today.

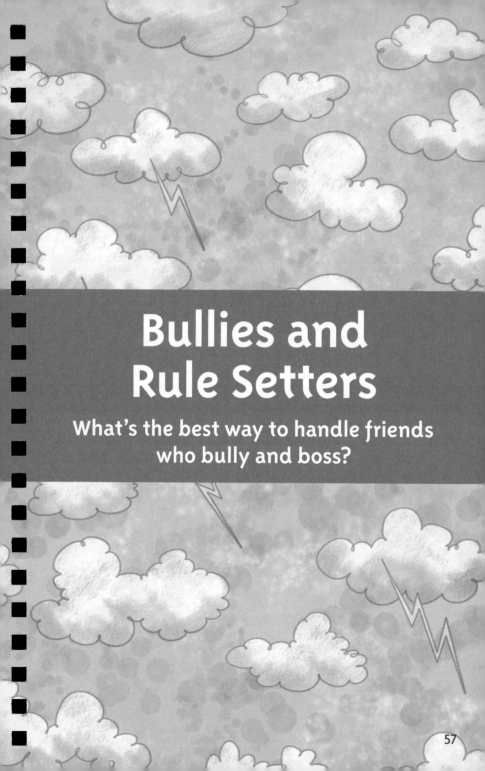

Bullies and Rule Setters

What's the best way to handle friends who bully and boss?

Nip Bullying in the Bud

What do you do when you see a friend bully someone—or worse yet, when she bullies you? Answer these questions to gauge how you react to the bullies in your life.

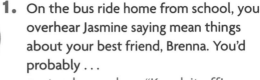

1. On the bus ride home from school, you overhear Jasmine saying mean things about your best friend, Brenna. You'd probably . . .
   a. stand up and say, "Knock it off! Don't talk about Brenna that way. Just because she's smarter than you doesn't mean she deserves to be talked about."
   b. say, "That was cold. I'm sitting right here, and Brenna is my best friend."
   c. act as if you didn't hear a thing—you don't want Jasmine to pick on you next!

2. You're playing Truth or Dare at a sleepover when Samara insists you do a dare that you don't feel comfortable with. "If you won't make that prank call," Samara barks, "I'll tell everyone at school you have lice." You'd probably . . .
   a. go ahead and make the call—you agreed to play, and those are the rules.
   b. say, "Hey, this game is supposed to be funny, not nasty. Let's play something else."
   c. snap back, "And I'll tell everyone that I got them from you."

3. Matilda gets you to join her online club. But she says that another friend, Terri, can't join. "She's on the chess team. What a geek!" Matilda crows. Matilda says she doesn't want to see you hanging around with Terri or you'll be out of the club, too. You'd probably . . .

    a. say, "Thanks, Matilda, but I can't be in your club if it's about keeping people out instead of getting people together."

    b. say, "Geez, there's no nice way to respond to that, so I won't."

    c. tell Terri that you just can't be friends with her anymore— you really want to be popular, and Matilda is popular.

4. Misty is the popular girl in your grade, and she seems to like you. She even invited you to a party at her house. But at the party, you see her putting down Jen, another friend. "Who let you in the door in that outfit?" Misty rudely says to Jen. You'd probably . . .

    a. tell Jen, "Hey, I like your outfit. I think you look great."

    b. act as if Jen is not your friend when you see her at the party.

    c. tell Misty, "That's rude. Does your mother mind if you talk like that?"

5. It's the first day of summer break, and you show up at the pool in your swim-team one-piece. But Alondra and her popular friends are all wearing bikinis this year. She says, "One-pieces are OUT! You look like a five-year-old in that." You'd probably . . .

    a. say, "But this suit gives me the speed I need to actually *win* on the swim team."

    b. run to the locker room and put your shorts and T-shirt back on. "I just want to sit in the sun," you say sheepishly when you come out.

    c. laugh and tell Alondra, "Thanks! Just the look I was going for."

Scoring

Give yourself 3 points for every orange answer you chose, 2 points for each green answer, and 1 point for each violet answer. Add up your score.

12 or more points: Power Flower

You don't let bullies push you or your friends around. You know that no one deserves to get bullied—ever. But avoid becoming a bully yourself. Pay attention to people's feelings. If you push too hard, you could keep the anger growing.

8 to 12 points: Olive Branch

You can see when you or a friend is being bullied, and you face the situation with humor or kindness. Standing up isn't easy, but you know that being polite and using a laid-back approach could solve the problem without upsetting people.

7 points or fewer: Shrinking Violet

You tend to turn away from trouble, but sometimes you may need to speak up. Ask a trusted friend or an adult to practice confronting bullies with you. You're right to want to avoid a hot situation, but if you don't stand up to bullies, who will?

Start!

A mean girl walks up to you, says, "I think you're really pretty," and then giggles snidely. You'd probably . . .

say, "And I think you're really nice."

say, "Hmmm . . . great!"

just walk away from her.

When a know-it-all student peeks at your score on the last math test and snarks, "How can you do so poorly in math?" you'd probably . . .

chuckle, "I don't do well at handling other people's problems."

sigh, "So I'm not a math whiz. Oh, well."

In the lunch line, a bully copies your every move, trying to make you look silly and feel uncomfortable. You'd probably . . .

just keep walking through the line, hoping she cuts it out.

ask, "Don't you have anything better to do?" Then keep moving.

You feel really stylish in your cute new hat. But then you hear a rude girl shout, "I can't believe you're wearing that!" You'd probably . . .

say back, "Believe it. And I happen to like it."

On the bus, the bully sitting behind you is holding her nose and pointing at you, acting as if you smell bad. You'd probably . . .

turn around and ask, "What is your deal?"

ignore her completely.

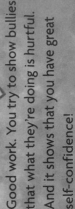

ignore her and not let her ruin how you feel about your new look.

Good work. You try to show bullies that what they're doing is hurtful. And it shows that you have great self-confidence!

BRAVO

Great! You like to deal with bullies by ignoring them or walking away. This lets the bully know that she can't take any power away from you.

Clever Comebacks

Choose your path toward telling bullies to buzz off!

Time to Tell?

No one wants to be a tattletale. And it's important to figure out how to handle bullies on your own. But sometimes you need to tell an adult what's going on. Imagine that each of the following situations happened to you. Then put a check in the bubble next to each one you'd make sure to discuss with an adult you trust.

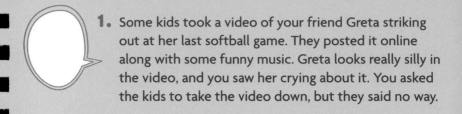

1. Some kids took a video of your friend Greta striking out at her last softball game. They posted it online along with some funny music. Greta looks really silly in the video, and you saw her crying about it. You asked the kids to take the video down, but they said no way.

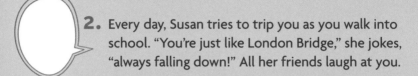

2. Every day, Susan tries to trip you as you walk into school. "You're just like London Bridge," she jokes, "always falling down!" All her friends laugh at you.

3. Rita makes a list of all the girls who can sit at the cool lunch table—and all the girls who can't. You hate it that she thinks she's in charge of everyone. Just yesterday, she made your friend Allie find another place to sit.

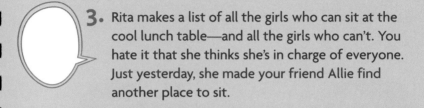

4. You get 100% on a really tough geometry test. Your teacher says you must be cheating—he tells you that a girl like you could never get such a good grade on her own.

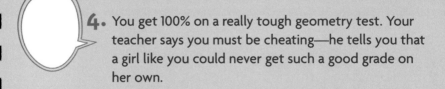

5. Your friend Maddie is overweight. Sasha made up a rude song about Maddie today and sang it quietly whenever Maddie walked by.

6. Alaina teases you because you bring your lunch to school instead of buying it at school. "Your family must be so poor!" she sneers.

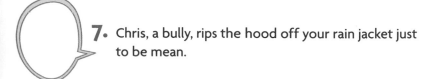

7. Chris, a bully, rips the hood off your rain jacket just to be mean.

8. You think that Sylvia is copying your answers on every history quiz. "If you ever tell," she hisses, "I'll spread a rumor that you went home the other day because you peed your pants at school." Really, you left for a dentist appointment.

Answers

1. Time to tell. It's not OK for Greta's image to be online without her parents' permission. Talk to Greta, and then go to the principal together.

2. Time to tell. If you've asked Susan to stop, and she repeatedly gets physical, you need to speak up.

3. Try to work it out. Don't let Rita boss you around. Tell her that you think what she's doing is mean, and tell her that you won't be a part of it. But if that doesn't work, offer to go with one of the ousted kids and talk to a counselor.

4. Time to tell. If you're bullied by an adult, always talk to another adult you trust, such as your parent or a school counselor.

5. Try to work it out. Be brave and tell your friend and the bully that it's not OK to tease people. If Sasha teases Maddie again, then it's time to tell.

6. Try to work it out. Tell the bully, "You don't need to worry about me. I'm doing just fine." Leave it at that and walk away. If she doesn't back off, time to tell.

7. Time to tell. Any time anyone is physical or hurts you, it's time to speak up.

8. Try to work it out. Ask your teacher if you can move away from Sylvia. Say that you're having trouble concentrating because Sylvia is bugging you.

Here's a useful rule:
If you are trying to make someone look bad, you're tattling.
If you're trying to help someone, it's telling.

65

Could You Be Bossy?

Among your friends, is there someone who bullies? Who's rude? Who always makes others do things her way? Take this quiz to find out if the bossy friend might be *you*.

1. You really want Gina to hang out at your house this Saturday. But she has plans with Ebony, another friend. "If you hang out with Ebony, then you don't really care about me," you say to Gina.

☐ That's me.

☐ No way.

2. Your friend Dora always wears gym shoes, but you think ankle boots are in. "I can't sit by you on the bus the next time you wear sneakers with a skirt," you say to Dora with a scowl.

☐ That's me.

☐ No way.

3. You're working on a group book report for English class with your friends Jane and Toni. "Toni, you read the book and make an outline. Jane, you make a poster about the book. I'll talk in class because I'm best at that," you say.

☐ That's me.

☐ No way.

4. You're with your friends at the mall, and you all decide to get soft pretzels. But you discover you're out of money. "Kayla, you've got to pay for me," you say.

☐ That's me.
☐ No way.

5. All the "in crowd" girls are talking about a party at Ashley's house this Friday. You'd love to go, but you didn't get an invite. So you post a message online telling all your closest friends not to attend. "Being popular is all she really cares about," you complain.

☐ That's me
☐ No way.

If you checked "That's me" for any of the questions, read on for some advice about how to banish your bossy behavior.

1. Using ultimatums as a way to manipulate your friends is really being bossy—and almost being a bully. It's OK to feel jealous about being left out, but if you're a great friend to Gina, she'll want to spend time with you again. A visit with Ebony won't change that.

2. Setting rules about what your friends can and can't do is a kind of bullying. It's fine to have opinions, but your friends don't have to share them to be your friends. A good friend keeps an open mind to the ways she differs from her pals.

3. Sometimes you can get your way by being the loudest or by making it known that you'll create a fuss if you don't get what you want. But that's bullying, too. So is taking credit for work you haven't done yourself. Treat your friends with respect. If you're working on a group project, make sure everyone gets a say in how the team will get the job done.

4. Trying to force friends to do what you want them to do is being the ultimate boss. Ask a friend nicely for a favor. The worst thing she can say is no—and there'll be no hard feelings.

5. Ease up. Trying to force your friends into doing anything can backfire—big time. You should never control a good friend. Respect her choices, and, hopefully, she'll respect yours.

All About You

What makes you fit in with your friends?

All Ears

You love to chat with your friends. But do you really hear what they have to say? To check in on your listening skills, put a check mark next to each statement that could describe you.

Your friends like to share private thoughts and feelings with you because they know you'll keep your lips zipped.

It's hard for you to wait for your turn to talk in a conversation. You often interrupt to make sure your point is heard.

A lot of times, you find yourself thinking about what you want to say next in a conversation instead of concentrating on what your friend is talking about.

You might send a text message to one friend while you're talking to another.

You like to look friends in the eye when they're talking to you.

When a friend tells a story, you think of questions you could ask to find out even more.

You don't usually feel as if you're the person who talks the most in a conversation.

When you talk on the phone with a friend, you make a point to stay focused on the conversation.

Problems often come up between you and your friends because of misunderstandings—your friends insist that they said one thing, but you're sure that they said something else.

When you chat with friends you know well, you often finish their sentences or say what you think they're going to say.

Your friends tell you that you're a good listener.

Sometimes when a friend talks, you pretend to listen, but you're really thinking about something else.

Answers

If you checked mostly **red** statements, you're tuned in to what your friends have to say. They like to talk with you because they know you'll value what they say even if you don't agree. Make sure that you get the chance to speak your piece, though. Don't let your friends take advantage of your generosity as a listener.

If you checked mostly **turquoise** statements, you need to polish up your listening skills. Don't worry—most people can improve the way they listen in conversation. Try to make one change at a time. For example, set a goal to give a friend you're talking to your undivided attention—whether you're chatting in person or on the phone. Or make a mental note not to decide how you feel about what a person is saying until she's made her entire point. Or use physical signs, such as nodding or smiling, to show that you're really listening.

Pressure Cooker

Do you always go along with the group—even when you're not sure it's the right thing to do? Take this quiz to find out how you handle peer pressure. Circle the answer that suits you best.

1. At parties, your friends Leanna and Hillary always want to dance. You hate dancing! You'd rather chat with friends or play video games. But you dance anyway. When you come to a party with your friends, you have to do what they want, right?

Sounds like me.

No way.

2. It seems as if all the girls in your school are wearing makeup this year. Your mom says you're not allowed to wear makeup, and you don't really like it anyway. But every morning on the bus, you put on some lip gloss. You just want to look like you fit in.

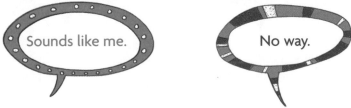

Sounds like me.

No way.

3. All your pals are trying out for volleyball. You like the sport, but the team practices at the same time you take horseback-riding lessons. "You've got to quit riding," your pal Sue Ellen complains, "or you'll miss out on everything!" You tell her that what you don't want to miss is your riding lessons.

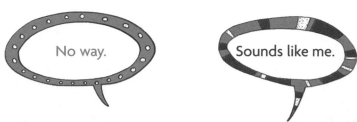

No way.

Sounds like me.

4. Your teacher takes your class to the library for a research session. She tells you and the other students to start your computers and wait until the librarian arrives. Then she leaves. Your classmates decide to sneak over and read the comic books instead of starting their work. You know it's wrong, so you decide to turn on your computer and wait.

No way.

Sounds like me.

5. On Fridays, you're allowed to order pizza at school. "The whole table is getting pepperoni!" pronounces your friend Coral. Pepperoni gives you a stomach ache, but you don't say anything. No one will notice if you don't eat much.

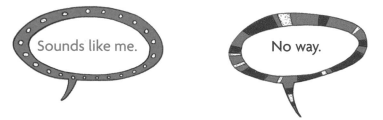

Sounds like me.

No way.

6. In middle school, you have to choose between choir and band. All your friends pick choir, but you've been taking trumpet lessons. You decide to join band, even though you don't know any of the other kids who play instruments.

7. You love scouting—you've been with your troop for five years. But this year some of your friends say that they feel too old for scouting. You stick with your troop anyway. You know you're a role model for the younger members, and you don't want to let them down.

Answers

If you picked mostly **purple** answers, peer pressure doesn't have too much power over you. You value your friends' ideas and opinions, but you find ways to do what you want or what you know is right without putting your friends down.

If you chose mostly **turquoise** responses, you tend to follow the crowd. The next time you feel pressured to do something you don't want to do, think of a way to follow your heart without hurting your friends' feelings.

Are You a Great Friend?

Answer these questions to see why you're a very valuable pal.

1. You having fun with your friends looks most like . . .

a.

c.

b.

2. A nice thing you'd do for a friend is . . .
   a. bring her homework to her when she has missed school.
   b. write a poem that describes all the things you love about her.
   c. send her an e-mail with a funny joke when you know she's been feeling down.

3. Your friends trust you because . . .
   a. you know how to keep a secret.
   b. you know how to keep a promise.
   c. you know how to keep them out of trouble.

4. You fit in with your friends by . . .
   a. making sure they have a good time when you get together.
   b. being someone they can depend on, no matter what.
   c. recognizing what's special about each one of them.

5. You'd stick up for a friend by . . .
   a. telling a bully who's bugging her to buzz off.
   b. cheering on her sports team.
   c. defending her when someone gossips behind her back.

6. Your friends like you because . . .
   a. you know how to make them laugh.
   b. you bring out the best in them.
   c. you accept them for who they are.

Take a look at your choices. Guess what? They're *all* right answers! There are so many different ways to be a first-rate friend. When problems do come up, be kind to your friends, be honest with them, and treat your friends the way you would like them to treat you. Stay true to yourself. You'll find friends who like you for the wonderful person you are!

Which was your favorite quiz? Tell us!

Mail to
Friends Till the End? Editor
American Girl
8400 Fairway Place
Middleton, WI 53562

Here are some other American Girl books you might like.